SPEAK WITH INFLUENCE

Craft, Pitch, and Impact:
The Ultimate Guide to
Landing Your Dream
TEDx Talk

DR. IZDIHAR JAMIL, PH.D.

BOOK REVIEWS

"Under the expert guidance of Dr. Izdihar Jamil, my TEDx talk underwent a transformative evolution. Dr. Jamil's expertise in simplifying complex concepts helped me seamlessly translate my ideas to the audience, making my talk more impactful. The journey with Dr. Jamil unfolded the art of distilling brilliance, shaping my TEDx talk authentically"
- Anjani Amriit, Expert Inner Development for Professional Impact

"In chapter three, Izdihar succinctly describes important components of an effective TEDx talk. As the organizer and curator of TEDx Huntington Beach 2023, she helped to make it a very successful event. Izdihar illustrates keys to creating an effective talk by citing examples from TEDxHuntingtonBeach"
- Dr. Jay Winner, MD, Medical Practitioner and TEDx Speaker

"Izdihar simplifies the process of crafting a TEDx Talk that follows the guidelines. Making TEDx Talks can be challenging because the speakers need to make them bitable and digestible within a short time while sharing their big ideas. Her book shows step by step for those who want to land their TEDx speech."

- Aiko Hemingway, TEDxHuntingtonBeach Speaker

"Izdihar sets such a high standards because she wanted us to be the best at what we do. She is methodological and clear in her process of taking our idea into something unique that will have a big impact on the audience. She cares about her speakers and works hard in making sure that our message and delivery is in the best shape"

- Laura Clancy, TEDxHuntingtonBeach Speaker

DEDICATION

To Yaya, the bravest and prettiest little girl. Thank you for teaching Mommy what it feels like to be brave. I know you'll be proud and courageous of your roots and heritage and will honor who you are.

To all of the women who dare to go the opposite direction—keep on your path, darlings!

BARRIERS

I know you're looking at me
But do you really see me?
Are you threatened?
Am I suspicious?
Because I look different

I know you're probably judging me
But these Whispers are misleading

I feel a shaking in my bones
Feel your Eyes cold as stone
If I run… will it ever change?

Barriers …. Barriers

Pushing through barriers
I got to change the way I see you
If you're ever gonna see me

Barriers …. Barriers

Pushing through barriers
We gotta love a little harder
We gotta hold each other stronger

I know you don't hear your words
Or the way that they hurt
As they're playing

Over and over and over again in my mind…

As my children find me
Laying on the floor
Tears streaming down my face
Trying to open up my heart to you

Barriers …. Barriers

Pushing through barriers
I got to change the way I see you
If you're ever gonna see me

Barriers …. Barriers

Pushing through barriers
We can't find the truth if we're hiding
We can't come together in the silence

Can we find the footsteps in the dark
To where there's nothing but love

Barriers …. Barriers

Pushing through barriers
I got to change the way I see you
If you're ever gonna see me

Barriers …. Barriers

Pushing through barriers
We can't find the truth if we're hiding
We can't come together in the silence

Pushing down barriers
Pushing down barriers
Breaking down barriers
Breaking down barriers

Song written by Izdihar Jamil and Drew Lawrence.

Music composed by Drew Lawrence.

Singer: Izdihar Jamil

TABLE OF CONTENTS

INTRODUCTION

"Leave a legacy. Create a Movement. That's your purpose to speak on the TEDx stage!"
- Dr. Izdihar Jamil

My friend Michelle says, "Izzy, you gotta speak on the TEDx stage." It's one of my biggest desires, but I told her I just had Rayhan, my third child, and I'm scared of public speaking. "I don't think I can do this!" Then she said, "You're a trailblazer. Where you go, people will follow. You want to create a path so that other people can share their voice."

There were many things that went through my mind. With a newborn baby, I didn't want to have another thing on my plate. Rayhan was seven years younger than Nadrah, my second child, and ten years apart from Abrar, my eldest. It's like I'm starting back to zero. The sleepless nights, the nursing, the nappy changes while taking care of Abrar and Nadrah and running a business. It was a LOT. But there was this pull, this yearning and burning desire that just wants to be heard. I didn't know if I had a TED-worthy idea yet, but this desire was so strong that I couldn't ignore it. A few days after, I took a leap of faith and decided to put myself out there for speaking on a TEDx stage.

I started to apply to several TEDx events and conferences in my area. Because of Rayhan, I knew I

1

only wanted to speak at my local TEDx events. I didn't want to have to travel out of town or out of state to speak. The pandemic was slowly subsiding, and I didn't want to take any unnecessary risks. I was faced with multiple rejections. After one rejection in particular, I called Michelle and just cried. It was heartbreaking to face rejection because I felt that I wasn't good enough. But deep down, I knew rejection was just God's protection. It is part of our process to course correct to our best path. Because of the multiple rejections, I learned a lot about what TEDx organizers want and how they filter their applicants. I started to get better and clearer on my TED-worthy idea, and that helped me a lot in standing out with my applications with the organizers. I kept on applying to various TEDx events until the perfect organizer, Sonali Fiske from TEDxDelthroneWomen, said, "YES!" to me, and I said, "YES!" back.

TEDxDelthroneWomen was the perfect place for me. I wanted somewhere close, and it was less than an hour's drive from home. It's a women-based event. I wanted to be involved where strong, powerful women were standing together to create a movement within a community. I wanted it to be an event with diverse backgrounds that showcased bold voices. TEDxDelthroneWomen aligned with my vision, and its theme was REVOLUTION- the perfect place for my TEDx idea to be heard.

My dream was to be the BEST TEDx speaker I could be. I sought help from the best experts in the industry from storytelling to stage performance and body movement. I practiced every day. While cooking my Malaysia curry noodle to when I'm driving to pick up the kids from school and missing turns along the way because I'm so focused on my new craft, even when I'm pushing Rayhan in the stroller I am practicing.

On the 4th of December, 2021, the day of my TEDx talk, I'm wearing a teal dress, a royal blue hijab, and a touch of Chanel perfume. I'm the ninth speaker out of twelve. The nerves are kicking in. I'm walking, stretching, praying, and meditating in the green room just to calm my nerves. Then the MC, Sonali Fiske, says, "Our next speaker is Dr. Izdihar Jamil, and what I love most about her is her smile." In that moment, I close my eyes and say, "God, just let me BE. Let them hear my heart. Help me touch their hearts. Help me to take care of one person so I can be so grateful." I open my eyes, look to my right, and smile at the audience as I'm walking up the stage. I stop at the red dot, turn to the audience, and say my first line: "My husband, Rizal, got his dream job!" I can see a world where my nine-year-old daughter, Nadrah, is going to grow up as a Muslim woman, and I don't like it. That's why I chose to share my voice on the TEDx platform.

I shared that the revolution to overcoming social adversity isn't to blend, change, conform, or transform yourself to fit the preconceived notion of society's checklist, but rather to be proud of your roots and heritage and to be courageously open and accepting of each other's differences. During my talk, I invited the audience to be proud and courageous of their roots and heritage. Revolution is about making bold moves, and I hoped that my talk had inspired them to do so. At the end of my talk, I received one of the loudest, and longest, standing ovations I could ever dream of. After my talk, people came to me and said, "You made me cry with your story!" "I wish my daughter was here to hear your story!"

My TEDx talk, "Coming to America: A Story of A Hijab Wearing Woman," now had over 100,000 views, and I received messages from people all around the world saying how my talk helped them to make courageous choices in their lives, to be proud of who they are, and to not settle into society's preconceived notions. It's such a magical feeling to know that, somehow, I was able to spark the seeds for bold movements and impacted others. This led me to curate and organize my own TEDx event, TEDxHuntingtonBeach, so I could create a platform where the voices of my community can be heard and understood. Hopefully, along the way, we can be a catalyst of impact and create a powerful movement of possibility.

Curating and organizing TEDxHuntingtonBeach, reviewing hundreds of applications, and coaching many speakers gave me valuable insights on how to help others land their dream TEDx talk. My belief is that if one person who speaks on the TEDx stage can have a significant or even a small but meaningful impact in inspiring others, then we can hopefully create an open and accepting society where Nadrah can live as a proud Muslim woman.

Book Structure

In this book, I will be peeling back the layers to the illusive world of TED and TEDx talks, a journey that will empower you to not only discover your most profound ideas but also deliver them in a way that leaves a lasting impact. As a TEDx speaker, curator, and organizer who has trained numerous TEDx speakers, this book is your personal roadmap to crafting the kind of talks that resonate with audiences and will unlock the doors to your dream TEDx stage.

What sets this book apart is its unique blend of insights from a TEDx curator who understands the intricacies of what makes a TED or TEDx talk truly exceptional. My goal is to provide you with the tools, techniques, and inspiration you need to speak with influence so you can convey your ideas effectively and make your voice heard on the TEDx stage.

Here's an overview of each chapter and what you will gain from reading them.

Chapter One: Why TED – TED's Guiding Light

A journey on understanding the heartbeat of TED. Uncover the mission that fuels the TEDx spirit. Dive into the elements that compose a captivating TEDx talk and explore the transformative effects it can have on both speaker and audience.

Chapter Two: TED vs TEDx – Embracing Local Brilliance

Discover the beauty of TEDx, the independently organized event of TED. Explore its community-centric nature, celebrating the power of local messages within a global platform. Unravel the unique dynamics that set TED and TEDx apart, yet unite them in a shared mission.

Chapter Three: The TEDx Talk Ingredients – Crafting Brilliance

Delve into the artistry of a TEDx talk. Learn the alchemy behind its length, the necessity of a unique idea, the infusion of a new lesson, and the transformative impact of a compelling call to action. Unpack the formula that turns an idea into a TEDx masterpiece.

Chapter Four: Use Your Passion – Igniting the Flame Within

Fan the flames of your passion with five dynamic methods: Identify, Mapping, Go Deep, Research, and

Synthesize. Unearth the essence of what truly drives you, laying the foundation for a TEDx-worthy talk that emanates authenticity.

Chapter Five: Leverage Your Expertise – Illuminating the Path

Illuminate your journey by drawing on your expertise. Learn how to teach something new, specific, or different, and uncover the process of finding your TEDx-worthy idea within the realms of your proficiency. Your expertise is the key to unlocking profound insights.

Chapter Six: Socio/Cultural Trends of Challenges – Riding the Waves of Change

Navigate the currents of socio-cultural trends and challenges. Learn to reflect, synthesize, and distill valuable lessons from the challenges of our times. Transform these insights into TED-worthy ideas that resonate with the collective consciousness.

Chapter Seven: Overcoming Adversity – Turning Pain into Power

Explore the profound lessons adversity can teach. Learn the guidelines for exploring personal adversity and understanding how the challenges you've faced can illuminate a path for others. Your story of triumph over adversity is a beacon of hope.

Chapter Eight: Challenging Assumptions and Thinking Disruptively – Breaking Chains of Thought

Break free from conventional thinking. Embrace the challenge of disrupting assumptions and perspectives. Explore radical solutions and dare to ask, "what if?" Challenge the status quo with the power of disruptive thinking.

Chapter Nine: Physical Limitations – Beyond Boundaries

Discover the positive propeller within physical limitations. Uncover what people may not know about the strength that lies beyond constraints. Learn how to craft a TEDx talk that transcends the physical, leaving a lasting impact.

Chapter Ten: Landing Your Dream TEDx Talk – Stand Out and Shine

Decode the secrets of what each TEDx organizer seeks. Understand the key elements that make your application shine. Uncover how to position yourself as the perfect fit for the TEDx stage, leaving organizers eager to have you share your idea.

Chapter Eleven: 5 Steps to Jumpstart Your TEDx Journey – Your Odyssey Begins

Embark on your TEDx journey with five essential steps: Brainstorm, Research, Understand What the

Organizer Needs, Submit Your Application, and Rehearse Your Talk. Each step propels you closer to the moment you step onto the TEDx stage, ready to share your powerful message. Your odyssey begins now.

As you navigate through these chapters, you will uncover the secrets of crafting talks that resonate, inspire, and ultimately land you on the coveted TEDx stage. With each section, you'll gain the knowledge, inspiration, and practical tools needed to share your TED-worthy ideas and make a lasting impact.

Are you ready to embark on this transformative journey?

The TEDx stage is calling, and this book is your guide to answering that call. By reading "Speak With Influence," you will gain a deeper understanding of what it takes to craft, pitch, and deliver ideas that truly matter, and you'll be equipped with the skills to make your dream TEDx talk a reality. Join me and other successful TEDx speakers on this adventure, and let's unleash the power of your ideas.

Let's begin your TEDx journey now.

CHAPTER ONE

Why TED - TED's Guiding Light

"TED is one of the most powerful and influential platforms in spreading thought provoking ideas in the world." - Dr. Izdihar Jamil

B efore you start brainstorming your TED-worthy idea, it is essential to understand the profound mission that TED embodies. You want to make sure that both your mission and TED's mission are in alignment so you can create ideas that are truly meaningful and profound.

"TED is on a mission to discover and spread ideas that spark imagination, embrace possibility and catalyze impact. Our organization is devoted to curiosity, reason, wonder, and the pursuit of knowledge — without an agenda. We welcome people from every discipline and culture who seek a deeper understanding of the world and connection with others, and we invite everyone to engage with ideas and activate them in your community."

- Source: https://www.ted.com/about/our-organization

TED's mission is to explore the wonder of knowledge in the hope that it will spark imagination, possibility, and be a catalyst for change. It is not for your own personal benefit, such as promoting your business, brand, social media, books, movies, courses, beliefs, or political agendas. It is about creating a movement and making an impact beyond what you could achieve by yourself.

The Power of Ideas

TED believes in the transformative power of ideas. It recognizes that a single idea, when shared and nurtured, has the potential to shape minds, challenge norms, and spark meaningful change. TED strives to showcase ideas that are innovative, thought-provoking, and capable of igniting conversations that transcend boundaries.

Social Engagement

At the heart of TED's mission lies a commitment to fostering social engagement. TED understands that great ideas have the capacity to connect people, inspire collective action, and address societal challenges. By providing a platform for individuals to share their insights, TED enables social discourse, encourages empathy, and promotes a deeper understanding of our shared humanity.

Value of Curiosity

TED cherishes curiosity as a driving force behind human progress. It celebrates the power of asking questions, exploring new frontiers, and challenging assumptions. TED nurtures a culture of inquiry, inspiring individuals to delve into diverse topics, disciplines, and perspectives. It encourages intellectual curiosity as a catalyst for personal growth and societal advancement.

Spreading Knowledge

TED is committed to the dissemination of knowledge and believes that it should be accessible to all. By sharing captivating talks through various platforms, including the TED.com website and TEDx events, TED democratizes learning and ensures that valuable insights reach millions of eager minds worldwide. TED empowers individuals with knowledge, enabling them to expand their horizons, deepen their understanding, and make informed decisions.

TED's mission revolves around the power of ideas, social engagement, the value of curiosity, and the spreading of knowledge. It serves as a beacon of inspiration, fostering intellectual growth, and bridging gaps between diverse communities. Aligning your idea with TED's mission can amplify your impact, as you become part of a global movement dedicated to inspiring, enlightening, and connecting individuals around the world.

Elements of a TED Talk

TED talks are not designed to be simply motivational or commercialized buy-from-me types of talks. They are built on the foundation of "ideas worth spreading" and aim to provoke thought, stimulate conversations, and inspire positive change. Here are several reasons why TEDx talks go beyond motivational or self-promotional speeches:

Ideas Worth Spreading

TED talks focus on presenting innovative, thought-provoking ideas that have the potential to make a significant impact on society. These ideas are carefully curated and selected to provide intellectual stimulation and promote critical thinking.

Thought-Provoking Conversations

TED talks aim to spark conversations and engage the audience in meaningful dialogue. The talks delve into deep, complex topics, challenging preconceived notions and encouraging individuals to think beyond their comfort zones. They strive to leave a lasting impression on the audience, prompting them to question, reflect, and explore new perspectives.

Avoiding Self-Agenda Promotion

TED talks are not a platform for self-promotion or sales pitches. While speakers may share personal stories or experiences, the focus is on the idea they present and the impact it can have on others. TEDx talks prioritize authenticity, integrity, and genuine contribution rather than using the stage solely for personal gain.

Teaching Something New, Different, or Specific

TED talks provide a platform for experts, innovators, and thought leaders to share their knowledge and expertise on a specific subject. The talks aim to educate and inform the audience about new discoveries, cutting-edge research, or unique insights. The focus is on providing valuable and tangible takeaways that expand the audience's knowledge and understanding. Equally as important, make sure that your topic is specific and not general. The clearer and more specific you are about your idea, the easier it will be to craft your talk within the limited time frame.

Inspiring a Call to Action

TED talks aim to leave the audience with a sense of inspiration and motivation to make a positive change in their lives or in society. Speakers often share actionable steps, practical advice, or compelling stories that ignite a desire for action. The talks encourage individuals to apply the ideas presented and take steps towards creating a better future.

TED talks transcend the realm of mere motivation or self-promotion. They embrace ideas worth spreading, engage in thought-provoking conversations, avoid self-agenda promotion, teach something new or specific, and leave the audience with an inspired call to action. By upholding these principles, TED talks have become a powerful platform for sharing innovative ideas, fostering dialogue, and inspiring positive change on a global scale.

TED Talk Effects

A TED talk is a powerful avenue to amplify your influence and make a lasting impact on society. If you consider yourself a thought leader who wants to make an enduring and profound impact on your community, then you should consider giving a TEDx talk.

My friend Dr. Masni is a prominent councilor at Universiti Sains Islam Malaysia (USIM), one of the top universities in Malaysia. She told me, "I love your TEDx talk, and I want you to come and speak at the University!" I was so happy to hear that from her and enthusiastically agreed. So, I flew out from Orange County, California, all the way to Malaysia to deliver the talk. On the day of the talk, Ayah, my dad, dropped me off at the University. Dr. Masni and I have been friends for years but haven't seen each other for so long. As we were catching up in the green room, five minutes before the event, the organizer said, "By the way, the audience only likes speakers who speak in either Malay or Arabic." I was like, "What?? Why didn't you tell me sooner!" I've prepared my entire three-hour talk in English. I'm a native Malay speaker and English is my first language, but to translate my entire three-hour talk from English to Malay in less than five minutes is totally bonkers!

It's not as easy as simply translating it word for word. Optimum translation should involve capturing the entire content without losing its meaning or essence. Proper translation would take days or even weeks of effort. I was panicking. "They are not going to like me! They are going to ask me to leave!" "They are going to say, 'Look at her, she's a Malay lady, and she's speaking English just to show off!'" One minute before the talk, I decided that I was going to stick to my plan and let the audience deal with me. Then the MC said, "I want to welcome to the stage Dr. Izdihar Jamil who flew all the way from California..." As I stepped on the stage and saw the faces of the audience in the auditorium, I took a deep breath and said my first line. "I was at a grocery store getting some dates when a guy asked me if I was going to blow myself up!"

Later that week, I got a call from the University. "Assalamualaikum, Dr. Iz. Are you available next week? We want you to come back and talk at an event!" I've been back to the University every year since and have had such great collaboration with them.

Since my TEDx talk, I've been blessed with many unexpected opportunities- clients, media coverage, a TV interview, speaking gigs, books, and collaborations. The success of TEDxHuntingtonBeach in training speakers and providing a platform for positive impacts on our communities is something that I didn't foresee when I gave my TEDx talk. My TEDx was the catalyst for so many events, relationships, and opportunities. When I did my TEDx talk, my goal was to help change the world so my daughter, Nadrah, could live in a society that's open and accepting of proud Muslim women. It wasn't so much about the glamor or credibility—It was for a cause that I believed in.

Many TEDx speakers that I've met did it for the spotlight; they wanted their pictures on the red dot and the "TEDx Speaker" title. But that's where their efforts died because they didn't do it for the greatest good. They were driven by egotistical purposes: their businesses, books, programs, and for personal benefit. Once their talk is released, they do nothing to leverage the talk. So how does that help TED's vision of spreading thought-provoking ideas that are catalysts to impact the community?

Of course, with being a TEDx speaker, all the credibility and shiny stuff are going to come along with it. It's all part of the package. It's a privilege to be a TEDx speaker and to have your talk featured on the TED platform. Still, there are BIGGER things than just the title or your picture on the red dot. You are in a position to be a catalyst for creating a powerful movement, so why not step into that role?

While I advocate for altruistic involvement in TED's platform and events, I think it is important to understand what can be gained by being a TEDx speaker. Hopefully, you can also see the possibility of creating a movement and leaving a legacy.

Credibility

Delivering a TED talk instantly bolsters your credibility. By sharing your unique insights on the TED stage, you solidify your reputation as an authority in your field. This heightened credibility can enhance your personal brand and open doors to new opportunities.

Authority

A TED talk provides a platform to showcase your expertise, establishing you as a thought leader in your domain. By sharing your original ideas, perspectives, and solutions, you have the opportunity to shape conversations, influence opinions, and drive change. Your TED talk becomes a testament to your mastery and positions you at the forefront of your industry.

Socio/Cultural Impact

TED talks have a remarkable ability to ignite conversations that transcend boundaries and impact society on a broader scale. By addressing pressing issues, presenting innovative solutions, or challenging the status quo, you can inspire change and cause others to take action. Your message can foster dialogue, shift paradigms, and contribute to the betterment of our socio-cultural fabric.

Legacy

Your TED talk becomes a powerful tool for leaving a lasting legacy. By sharing your wisdom, experiences, and vision, you immortalize your ideas and insights in a way that continues to inspire and influence future generations. Long after your talk is delivered, it becomes a resource for individuals seeking knowledge and guidance, ensuring your impact endures.

Exposure

Delivering a TEDx talk offers unparalleled worldwide exposure to your message and work. With the TEDx YouTube channel boasting over 38 million subscribers and TED.com attracting millions of loyal followers, your talk becomes accessible to a global audience hungry for thought-provoking ideas. This vast reach ensures that your message transcends geographical or political boundaries, allowing you to create genuine transformation for individuals from all corners of the world.

Inspired Action

A TED talk allows you to inspire and motivate others on a deeply personal level. Through engaging storytelling, you can ignite a sense of curiosity, hope, courage, fun, adventure, curiosity, and generosity in your audience. Your words become a catalyst for personal transformation, encouraging individuals to step out of their comfort zones, embrace new possibilities, and pursue their passions.

Embrace this opportunity to share your ideas worth spreading, and together, let us inspire and shape a brighter future.

CHAPTER TWO

TED vs TEDx- Embracing Local Brilliance

I am often asked what is the difference between TED and TEDx talks. The two platforms share a common vision of spreading ideas worth sharing, yet each possesses its own unique magic.

1) TEDx: Independently Organized, Community-Centric

The "x" in TEDx stands for independently-organized events, and this is where the magic begins. Imagine someone like me, driven by a vision of creating a space for the voices of my community, to be heard and understood. I curated the TEDxHuntingtonBeach event, focusing on bringing the voices of my community to the spotlight and addressing issues they are passionate about. TEDx is about local voices, local stories, and the local community.

When we left Malaysia to support my husband's dream job, we landed in Orange County, California. My kids went to school in Huntington Beach. We love it here, from the local grocery store, to the library, the parks, and the beach. If you have ever been to

Huntington Beach, you'll notice that it's a vibrant multicultural city. Because Huntington Beach is my first connection in America, it will always have a special connection to it.

I wanted to highlight the different voices, ideas, and issues of our new home to create a movement that could spark a world of possibility within my community. When I did my TEDx talk in 2021, sharing my unique idea of overcoming adversity as a hijab-wearing Muslim woman, I wanted to continue with the magic that I experienced when I had the freedom to share my voice and impact others.

Each TEDx event is different in its vision. I want you to consider going beyond the fame, glory, brand, or business benefits to create worthy content that can last for hundreds of years. Applying to organize TEDxHuntingtonBeach was scary- I had no funding, team, or speakers. But I had faith in my vision, and soon after, TEDxHuntingtonBeach was born.

2) TEDx Organizers Operate Under TED Brand and Guidelines

While TEDx events are independently organized, they operate under the umbrella of the TED brand and adhere to TED's guidelines. This ensures a consistent quality of talks and helps maintain TED's reputation for spreading thought-provoking ideas. It's a beautiful synergy where local passion meets global expertise. Adhering to the TED guidelines is important so that the content curated not only has the possibility to be a catalyst of impact but also ensures that it is free from any monetary, political, or religious agendas.

3) Committed, Passionate Volunteers

TEDx organizers and team members are the unsung heroes of our community. They are a diverse group of individuals, each with their unique backgrounds and talents, but bound together by a shared commitment to making a positive impact. These volunteers work tirelessly, fueled by their passion for ideas and the desire to create change at the local level.

Erin and I first met at Lakewood Ice, when Erin's sons, Thiery and Huntington, and my son, Abrar, played ice hockey for the same team. Our first conversation was, "Which one is your kid?" The majority of our interactions were screaming, cheering, and yelling at the top of our lungs while our kids played the game. Then our conversation shifted to asking each other what we do. Erin shared that she's a business strategist in a globally recognized company and mentioned that she was planning a mini-retirement. I shared with her that I help people to become bestselling authors and speak on the TEDx stage.

Little did I know that Erin is a fan of TED talks, and she asked me to share mine, "Coming to America: A story of a Hijab Wearing Woman." I shared that I gave my TEDx talk on social adversity and sent her the link and she loved it! Somehow, I found the courage to ask her, "Do you want to help me organize the TEDxHuntingtonBeach talk?" I realized I had nothing to lose by asking and so much to gain.

Thankfully, she said, "YES!" Since then, Erin has been a valuable asset to the team, taking care of the speakers and event coordination. She supported me when things got tough and held me accountable in being nurturing and professional throughout the process. It takes a lot to organize a TEDx event with an endless supply of unique details and requires doing a myriad of thankless jobs! She helped to make a lot of things happen without complaint.

In the book POSSIBILITY, that I curated with the team and speakers from TEDxHuntigntonBeach, Erin shared how she saw the TED speakers as brave. She also shared that saying 'YES' to TEDxHuntingtonBeach was way out of her comfort zone from the corporate world. But she decided to walk hand in hand with me. What was interesting was that a lot of her corporate skills were transferable in organizing TEDxHuntingtonBeach. So quick tip: never underestimate your existing skills and experience!

Working together for TEDxHuntingtonBeach in creating a world of POSSIBILITY has expanded us beyond our comfort zone and, in time, revealed our strengths and character. I love working with her because she shows up when she says she's going to show up, she delivers on results, and she is in alignment with the vision of creating the BEST event that will make a powerful impact.

If you are driven by ego in creating this event or want to be a speaker because of your brand, business, or superficial intentions, you will not last. The process will demand more from you: greatness at all levels. The question is, are you ready to hold yourself to a higher standard?

4) Local vs. Global Focus

TED is a global brand, known for its flagship conferences featuring speakers and topics from around the world. It takes a broad, global approach, tackling a wide range of topics. On the other hand, TEDx events are all about highlighting the voices and movements within a specific community or region. They serve as a platform for local changemakers to share their insights and inspire action at the grassroots level.

For the TEDxHuntingtonBeach 2023 Speaker Cohort, we had 12 speakers, some from our locality, some from out of state, and some from other countries. Because our theme is POSSIBILITY, all of the speakers were focused on delivering key messages surrounding the theme, making the message of the event both a local and a global focus.

5) From Curators to Producers

In the TEDx world, the organizer wears many hats. They are responsible for curating the speakers, defining the theme, securing sponsorships, and producing the entire event from start to finish. It's a labor of love, a symphony of passion and dedication that culminates in the magic of a TEDx event.

While adhering to the TED guidelines, I love the freedom that I have in curating my vision. The freedom to choose my own team members, for example, is important because I want to work with people that I like, are reliable and trustworthy. I don't want to have a big team. I want a small but mighty team, working with people who I trust and that'll deliver results.

I'm also appreciative of the opportunity to choose my own theme and speakers, allowing us the flexibility to work only with speakers that align to the vision, values, and mission of the event. It makes a huge difference when working with authentic and genuine people who play for a bigger goal than just being famous and promoting their business.

In the end, whether you're in the grand auditorium of a TED conference or the cozy setting of a TEDx event, the spirit of ideas worth sharing unites us all. TEDx gives a local voice to those whose stories might otherwise remain untold, while TED brings global perspectives that enrich our understanding of the world. Together, they form a tapestry of inspiration that spans the globe, reminding us that ideas are the currency of progress.

So, as you navigate this world of TED and TEDx, remember that it's not just about the stage or the spotlight; it's about the profound impact of ideas and the extraordinary people who dare to share them. In the end, it's a celebration of the human spirit, where each voice, whether local or global, plays a vital role in shaping our shared narrative of possibility and change.

CHAPTER THREE

The TEDx Talk Ingredients: Crafting Brilliance

"TEDx talk aren't just about inspiring or motivating others but teaching others something unique, specific, or different that can make an impact on their lives!" - Dr. Izdihar Jamil

TED's mission is to "*Make great ideas accessible and spark conversation.*" When coming up with ideas, speakers often mistake TED and TEDx talks for simply an inspiring and motivational speech. In a successful TED or TEDx talk, the speaker is able to teach the audience something new, specific, or different, and they walk away with a sense of curiosity and are inspired to take action.

In her TED talk, "Looks aren't everything. Believe me, I'm a model," Cameron Russell, a well-known supermodel, shared that beauty that is seen on magazines or in the media is orchestrated by many different specialists- makeup artists, stylists, photographers, and lighting experts. The beauty that we see isn't real beauty. Her idea is to accept your beauty as is instead of aspiring to the constructed beauty that we see in the media. This is a powerful idea that encourages conversations about the perception of beauty.

As the TEDxHuntingtonBeach curator and organizer, I want to share with you the guidelines for delivering an effective TEDx talk. These guidelines ensure that speakers provide captivating and meaningful experiences for the audience.

Length

TEDx talks should be between 7 to 10 minutes in duration. This time frame allows speakers to deliver their message concisely and ensures that the audience remains engaged throughout the entire talk. It challenges speakers to distill their ideas to their essence, delivering a powerful impact within a limited timeframe.

What I have noticed is that over time, TED and TEDx talks are becoming shorter and shorter as people's attention spans become less focused on long talks. Even the TED team is encouraging speakers to share their unique ideas in the shortest time possible (currently, we are encouraged to curate talks between 8-10 minutes) in the hopes that their messages are being heard instead of ignored based on the attention of the audience.

In 2023, we invited the speakers at TEDxHuntingtonBeach to speak a maximum of 9 minutes, which is a totally different approach when you've been asked to deliver a 45-minute keynote speech. Giving a 9-minute talk requires clarity, simplicity, and keeping only the important things.

During our virtual rehearsal, Anjani's talk was over the 9-minute threshold even though she was speaking very fast. Anjani was one of the speakers at TEDxHuntingtonBeach in 2023. One of the pointers that I'd given her was to slow things down and allow the audience to digest her point of view. Then I asked her to reflect on what's truly important. What will make her idea on tapping into your higher intelligence as an access to possibility and innovation shine?

A week later, we had another round of mini-rehearsal, and Anjani nailed her talk in less than 9 minutes! She wasn't rushing, and she has simplified and eliminated parts of her talk that may not have had the highest potential in sparking possibility, but she kept the parts that did. She delivered her TEDx on September 23rd, 2023 at TEDxHuntingtonBeach. It is a 7-minute talk; that's the power of simplicity, rehearsing, and openness to coaching.

Clear & Simple Ideas

Every TEDx talk should center around a clear and simple idea. The concept should be easily comprehensible and relatable to the audience. Speakers should articulate their ideas with clarity, avoiding jargon or unnecessary complexity. A straightforward and focused idea allows the audience to grasp and remember the key takeaway.

Selina, a speaker at TEDxHuntingtonBeach, had the idea of a life of sobriety after years of addiction, alcoholism, and mental health illnesses. There was a point, the lowest in her life, when she thought that her life was going to end. She wanted to let people know that it is possible to break through addiction. Selina is an example of that. She is now an incredible mother of three, an entrepreneur, and was the first cover model for a prestigious health magazine.

In one of our coaching calls, I asked her something like, "What is so unique about your journey of sobriety?" She said something like, "Having the right mindset." Then I asked her, "What kind of mindset?" Giving a TEDx or TED talk isn't about a general, common, or a vague idea. You want to have a clear and simple idea that is unique and comes from your own experiences.

As Selina worked through her talk, she discovered that her life of sobriety was possible because she never let herself be comfortable, and she used that drive to help others be uncomfortable in going after their dreams. Now, that's something unique, clear, and simple.

Specific and Deep

By delving into the intricacies of a specific topic, you can provide a more in-depth exploration and offer valuable insights that captivate the audience's attention. Going deep versus going broad and general, allows for a nuanced understanding, provokes thought, and fosters meaningful conversations. It ensures a more focused and impactful delivery, enabling the audience to gain profound knowledge and engage in a richer learning experience.

Aiko, who is one of the speakers at TEDxHuntingtonBeach in 2023, was told multiple times that her dream couldn't come true because her English wasn't good enough. She is originally from Japan but moved to America over 20 years ago.

For many years, she stopped pursuing her dreams. Then she decided to jump back in and went for her dreams. In her journey, she discovered how adults who are non-native speakers can learn a second language using vibration, energy, and breath.

This is something specific and deep because she isn't just talking about a general method but specifically using vibration: something that she discovered in her journey. In her talk, Aiko explains what it means to use vibration, breath, and energy to learn a second language as an adult. Learning a new language as an adult isn't just about figuring out the sounds of the words or the mouth movement when pronouncing the words, it's about how the words feel and the resonance of it when speaking it. This gives her talk a unique edge.

Storytelling

Effective TEDx talks utilize storytelling as a powerful tool to connect with the audience emotionally. By weaving personal anecdotes, narratives, or compelling examples into their talk, speakers create an emotional connection that captivates and resonates with the audience. Stories evoke empathy, engage the audience's imagination, and enhance the overall impact of the message.

Drew who is one of the speakers at TEDxHuntingtonBeach is an award winning, singer/songwriter who has worked with the biggest names in the industry like Leona Lewis, Christina Perry, and my personal favorite, the Backstreet Boys.

Drew opened up his talk singing the song that he wrote for Christina Perry, "Jar of Hearts,": "Who do you think you are? Running around leaving scars..." In his talk, he told multiple layers of stories, some personal and others people's stories, which brought a sense of magnetism to his talk and captivated the audience's attention.

Drew talked about how Christina Perry used her personal story, a story of heartbreak, to write a song with a powerful message to other women about not letting guys mess around with them. He also told a story about one of his clients, Pam, who wrote a song about her mother battling an illness.

Personal stories have the power to connect with the audience and create trust, warmth, and intimacy. I personally recommend including a personal story in your talk; it'll definitely add a beautiful layer to it.

However, you want to be mindful not to have all of your TEDx talk based on personal stories. Your talk needs to have a combination of other ingredients, such as learning, statistics, a call to action, your clear and simple idea, and storytelling, as outlined in this chapter.

Learning

A successful TEDx talk leaves the audience with new insights or perspectives. Speakers should aim to teach the audience something they may not have known before or present a novel approach to a familiar topic. By sharing fresh ideas, different, unique research findings, or innovative solutions, speakers stimulate curiosity and foster a thirst for knowledge.

Jay Winner, MD is another speaker at TEDxHuntingtonBeach. He's a family physician who, for many years, has been working with this community to encourage health and wellness. His talk is about how mindfulness can be the founding principle of a healthy lifestyle.

Jay talked about the six healthy lifestyles but focused on nutrition aspects and how mindfulness can be applied to them. In the talk, Jay can be seen holding a banana and then describing and eating the banana as part of his mindfulness demonstration.

This leaves his audience with a learning experience on how they can incorporate mindfulness in their nutrition or eating habits because they are shown a vivid and clear example of Jay eating his banana.

Impact

The talk should highlight the broader socio-cultural impact of the speaker's idea and emphasize its relevance to the audience's lives. By addressing the "why" behind the idea's significance and how it relates to the audience's experiences, aspirations, or challenges, speakers create a compelling case for the audience to care deeply about the topic. Consider the questions, "So what?" and "How can this idea benefit the audience?" to help sell and convince the audience of why they should listen to the talk.

Laura, one of the speakers at TEDxHuntingtonBeach, has a unique idea on how to bridge the gap between comedy and tragedy before tragedy even happens. Laura has suffered two floods and one fire in her home, and she found that finding laughter and comedy can often serve as a relief during those tough times.

One of the things that she said was how the discovery of Charlotte, a raccoon living in her house, and then a picture of a raccoon eating crispy fries on Facebook somehow has a spiritual meaning and letting her know that everything is going to be okay and that she's moving in the right pathway. She calls it the F.R.I.E.S. method.

One of the possible impacts that Laura's talk had on others is to find some form of comedic relief during a tragedy, and by following her F.R.I.E.S. method, those tragedies can lead to something greater in people's lives.

The No-No

TEDx talks should refrain from overtly promoting personal agendas, selling products or services, engaging in political discourse, or advocating for specific religious beliefs. The focus should stay on the sharing of ideas that inspire, educate, and engage the audience in meaningful ways.

As a curator, I often remind my speakers not to promote any personal products, services, businesses, or political and religious agendas. All of the speakers at TEDxHuntingtonBeach signed an agreement on this to ensure that they were in alignment with TED's mission.

Of course, as a business owner myself, I understand the need to promote and sell products and services, but the TEDx stage isn't the place for it. It is for a cause of socio-cultural impact; something that is way bigger than your own ego.

It is also off-putting to the audience when they are trying to learn something new to be pushed into a sales pitch. Speakers who promote their businesses, products, books, services, and political or religious agendas often don't see their TED talks accepted.

Let go of your ego and focus on what's important. Understand what iTED's and the TEDx organizer's missions are and see if you're in alignment with those visions. If you are not in alignment with TED's vision, perhaps the TED or TEDx stage isn't the place for you.

Connection and Relevance

An engaging talk establishes a connection with the audience from the beginning. Speakers should demonstrate an understanding of their audience's interests, concerns, or aspirations, and frame their talk in a way that resonates deeply with them. By establishing relevance, speakers create an immediate rapport, fostering an environment where the audience is eager to listen and learn.

Lisa is one of the speakers at TEDxHuntingtonBeach. She shares her unique idea on how to live a regret-free life by using your portable root system. She started off her talk about one of her former patients, who was 80 years old, who shared with her his wisdom on what a great marriage looks like. Lisa also talked about how moving to Canada from America after a whirlwind romance with her husband, Eric, led her to depend on her portable root system to live her best life.

At the end of her talk, Lisa walked her audience through a mini-meditation on creating a strong roots, just like trees, and how our roots can be connected and intertwined with each other. Lisa suggests that at any moment, we can tap into our own portable roots or the collected roots as we live our lives in a world of possibility. The mini-meditation creates a connection between Lisa and her audience as well as between the audience themselves who was there at the event and hopefully those watching on video too.

By adhering to the specified length, focusing on a clear and simple idea, utilizing storytelling, teaching something new, emphasizing socio-cultural impact, avoiding personal agendas, and establishing a connection with the audience, speakers can create impactful talks that inspire, educate, and foster meaningful change.

Statistics

While storytelling engages the heart, integrating statistics taps into the analytical side of our brains, creating a compelling balance. Imagine your talk as a well-rounded masterpiece – the art of storytelling combined with the science of statistics.

Statistics not only fortify your narrative but also lend credibility to your perspective. Selecting the right statistics from reputable sources, such as studies by organizations like the World Health Organization or surveys conducted by leading institutions, can elevate your talk. It's not about drowning your audience in numbers; it's about strategically placing statistics like building blocks to strengthen your message.

Remember, relevance is key. Choose statistics that seamlessly intertwine with your narrative, adding depth and nuance. Think of statistics as the supporting actors in your talk, enhancing the overall performance. So, when you craft your TEDx talk, consider the magic of statistics – a powerful tool to captivate minds and leave a lasting impact.

In her TEDx talk, Jen Fontanilla, who was one of the speakers at TEDxHuntingtonBeach added several statistics to support her claims that creatives and artists should change their money stories and that the saying "You're not going to make money as an artist" is invalid. Her statistics highlights the demand for creatives in the job industry and what creatives are making. The statistics mentioned are from reputable sources and are relevant to her talk, making her talk strong and credible.

Emotions

Let's dive into the art of injecting emotion into your talk – the secret sauce that transforms your presentation from mundane to memorable. Picture your talk as a rollercoaster of emotions, taking your audience on a captivating journey.

Sharing your personal experiences, like Selina did, creates a genuine connection with your audience. Be authentic in expressing the highs and lows of your journey, whether it's a triumph over adversity or the joy of achieving a milestone. Emotions serve as the heartbeat of your talk, resonating with your audience on a deeper level.

Remember, moderation is key. Like adding spice to a dish, sprinkle emotions throughout your talk without overwhelming your audience. Selina's talk beautifully balanced the gravity of addiction with the elation of overcoming it. Acknowledge the pain, but don't dwell on it – instead, use it as a stepping stone towards hope and resilience.

Humor is a fantastic tool to engage your audience but be mindful of appropriateness. A well-timed joke can create a positive atmosphere, fostering connection and understanding.

In her talk, Laura, when Laura talked about her discovery of her F.R.I.E.S. method, one of the first things that she said was something like, "First, I wanted French Fries..." and that caused the audience to laugh because it was something unexpected.

Gauge the emotional temperature of your audience and adjust your expression accordingly. Then, share your emotion with the audience, but remember not to overdo it.

Rehearsal

The stage is your canvas, and your TEDx talk is the masterpiece. The secret ingredient? Practice, practice, practice!

Don't procrastinate; start rehearsing from day one. Even if your talk is a work in progress, get those ideas flowing. Imagine practicing just 30 minutes a day – in a month, you've invested 900 minutes, and in five months, it's nearly 5000 minutes of refining your talk. Imperfect actions beat perfect intentions every time.

Engage with your audience early. Practice in front of friends, family, or colleagues. Their feedback is gold. You can sift through their insights and decide what enhances your talk. It's like fine-tuning a melody – each note matters.

Stage presence is crucial. If possible, practice on a stage. Familiarize yourself with the physicality of delivering your talk in the TEDx spotlight. Rehearsing on a stage helps you own that space, making the actual day feel like a familiar stroll rather than a nerve-wracking leap.

Here's the real magic – committed rehearsal turns your talk into second nature. On the big day, your hard work pays off, and your delivery is smooth, effortless, and impactful. So, don't just dream of delivering an exceptional TEDx talk; rehearse it into reality starting right now.

Give a Talk, Not a Performance

Treat your talk like a talk, not a performance. Unlike a theater audience, your TEDx audience is here for thoughtful ideas and meaningful insights, not a theatrical show.

I've witnessed many TEDx speakers transform their talks into performances, but here's the scoop – that's not what TEDx is about. Overperforming can kill the buzz and create a disconnect with your audience. Picture this: What wins over an audience is you talking to them like they're your best friend.

Think about it. When you chat with your best friend, do you slip into acting mode, or do you create a connection and share insights intimately? The answer is clear: Your TEDx talk should feel like a genuine conversation, a heart-to-heart with your audience.

So, ditch the theatrics and embrace the art of talking. Share your ideas authentically, like you're unraveling a fascinating story to your closest confidant. Let your passion, authenticity, and warmth shine through. That's the winning formula to captivate your TEDx audience and leave them with a lasting imprint. It's not a performance; it's a conversation with friends – make it count!

Call To Action

Call To Action is like wrapping up a fantastic date and not forgetting to ask for that second one. Leaving your audience without a call to action is like a missed opportunity.

Think of it as extending an invitation – an invitation to a realm of possibilities that your idea unlocks. You've taken your audience on a journey, and now it's time to guide them toward inspired action. Imagine going on a date, having a blast, and then not being asked for a second one – that's how your audience might feel without a clear call to action.

Keep it simple yet powerful. In my TEDx talk, "Coming to America: A Story of a Hijab-Wearing Woman," my call to action was to "Be proud and courageous of your roots and heritage." Anjani urged her audience to "Stop, pause, and do something different," while Drew inspired action with "Share the joy and the music inside of you today."

Your call to action is the bridge between your idea and the audience's action. It's the spark that ignites change. So, when crafting your call to action, think of it as the grand finale – a compelling invitation that propels your audience to carry your idea forward. Leave them inspired, motivated, and ready to embark on the next chapter ignited by your words.

You can check out the talks from the speakers who spoke at TEDxHuntingtonBeach at www.tedxhuntingt onbeach.com.

CHAPTER FOUR

Use Your Passion - Igniting the Flame Within

"Your passion for your topic will guide you in crafting the best TEDx talk that'll have the biggest impact on the community" - Dr. Izdihar Jamil

One of the things that most TED speakers have in common is that they are passionate about their topic. Just look at speakers such as Brené Brown, Cameron Russell, Bryan Stevenson, Scott Mann, and others.

Exploring your passions and interests is the key to unearthing TED-worthy ideas. When we dive deep into subjects that truly ignite our curiosity, we embark on a journey of boundless exploration and discovery. By immersing ourselves in these areas, we unlock a world of endless possibilities.

Passions drive us to seek knowledge, to understand and unravel the complexities of the world around us. They propel us towards new frontiers, where ideas converge, and innovation thrives. By actively engaging with our interests, we open doors to transformative insights and groundbreaking concepts.

Our passions act as beacons, guiding us through uncharted territory. They encourage us to traverse interdisciplinary landscapes, where fields intersect, and knowledge intertwines. Through this intersection, we forge unique connections, uncover novel perspectives, and unlock the true potential of our ideas.

In this pursuit, you must challenge assumptions and embrace disruptive thinking. By questioning the status quo and daring to explore unconventional paths, we set the stage for audacious ideas to flourish. Our passions empower us to think beyond the limitations of the familiar, propelling us toward innovative solutions and breakthroughs.

As we immerse ourselves in our chosen areas of interest, we become avid researchers, collectors of data, and analyzers of information. We tirelessly seek evidence and delve into the depths of knowledge. This rigorous approach allows us to identify gaps, uncover new insights, and generate TED-worthy ideas grounded in credibility and expertise.

Ultimately, exploring our passions and interests serves as the catalyst for the creation of TED-worthy ideas. By embracing our innate curiosity, challenging established norms, and immersing ourselves in research and analysis, we embark on a transformative journey. We become agents of change, armed with the power to inspire, educate, and ignite a fire within others.

5 Ways to Explore Your Passion

Here are five steps to explore your passion and interests to develop a TED-worthy idea. By following these steps, you will unlock the potential within yourself to inspire and captivate audiences with your innovative concepts.

Step 1: Identify

Begin by identifying the subjects or areas that genuinely excite you. Reflect on what truly sparks your curiosity and motivation. Ask yourself, "What topics ignite a fire within me?" By pinpointing these areas, you lay the foundation for uncovering ideas that resonate deeply with your passions.

If you're stuck in finding an area that you're truly excited about, some of the ways that have worked with me in getting unstuck is by incorporating movement in nature. I love going to the beach and just simply listening to the waves and breathing the salty air. It helped me calm my mind and just allow things to surface.

Prayers and meditation are also an effective way for me to seek guidance in finding my voice and passion. I would ask God to guide me in the path that'll seek my highest level of contribution for the highest good. In meditation, I'll just do a simple breath meditation where I'll focus on my breath: the ins and outs of my breathing. Often, it's hard for me to quiet my mind, so I'll just allow anything to show up but keep on focusing on my breath.

Talking to my friends, trusted friends, and colleagues, that is, people who will support my dreams, can be a game changer in finding ideas or brainstorming things in my life. I love listening to their point of view and ideas. Ultimately, remember that you're the one who gets to make the decision based on what feels true to you.

Step 2: Mind Map

Create a mind map to visualize your interests and explore their interconnectedness. This technique allows you to visualize the relationships between different topics and identify potential avenues for exploration. Map out the branches and subtopics, tracing the threads that weave through your areas of curiosity.

I like to set a timer for a short period of time. I'll set a timer for 15 minutes and then just brain-dump everything I can think of. Having a limited amount of time forces urgency and, therefore, triggers the brain to dump things out.

Then, I'll take a moment to review things and see if there's any direction that I want to explore further. I'll then set the timer for another 15 minutes and brainstorm that new direction. The key here is going more specific and deeper in a particular direction that I'm pulled towards.

Keep on doing that for a couple of times and notice things that come up in directing you towards a particular set of idea for your TEDx talk.

Step 3: Go Deep

Dive deeper into your chosen topics by listing the reasons why you are passionate or curious about them. Explore the personal and emotional connections you have with these subjects. What drives your curiosity? What impact do you believe these topics can have on society? By delving into your motivations, you will uncover the core values that fuel your ideas.

Giving a TEDx talk isn't about a general, inspiring speech. It's about focusing on a topic and then going deep and specific about it. Because TEDx talks are 10 minutes or less, you don't have the time to go broad about a topic. Nailing down your idea to something specific will help you to give a compelling talk in a short timeframe because you will not be distracted by things that are not important or relevant to the talk.

Step 4: Research

Conduct thorough research on existing TED talks related to your areas of interest. Analyze the perspectives presented and seek out unique angles or untapped aspects. By understanding the existing discourse, you can identify gaps or opportunities to propose a fresh perspective. Your TED-worthy idea should offer a new lens through which to view the topic, providing a captivating and thought-provoking experience for the audience.

Step 5: Synthesize

Synthesize all the insights and inspirations gathered from your exploration. Combine your own personal experiences, values, and research findings to craft a compelling narrative. Your idea should showcase a unique perspective that challenges conventional thinking or offers an innovative solution. By presenting your idea with clarity and passion, you can capture the attention and imagination of the TED audience.

By following these five steps - identifying your passions, creating a mind map, understanding your motivations, researching existing TED talks, and proposing a unique perspective - you will embark on a transformative journey of exploration. Through your TED-worthy idea, you will have the power to inspire, educate, and make a lasting impact on the world.

Case Study

Let's know dive into Drew Lawrence TEDx talk process, He's an award-winning singer/songwriter and a speaker at TEDxHuntingtonBeach, is a prime example of how passion can drive the creation of a TEDx talk that inspires and empowers others. With an unwavering love for music and a desire to help people tap into their creativity, Drew embarked on a journey to share his passion for songwriting and its connection to personal stories.

Driven by his own experiences and the transformative power of music in his life, Drew recognized the potential for individuals to express themselves through songwriting. In his TEDx talk, he embarked on a mission to teach people how to harness the power of their life stories to write meaningful and impactful songs.

Drawing from his vast knowledge and expertise, Drew honed in on a unique approach to songwriting by encouraging individuals to tap into their sensorial life experiences. He emphasized the importance of engaging the senses—smell, touch, feel, and see—to ignite creativity and evoke emotions that can be channeled into their songs.

By encouraging his audience to reflect on their personal experiences and the moments that resonated deeply with them, Drew provided a roadmap for translating those emotions into songs and lyrics. He guided them to think about the vivid details and the sensations associated with their experiences, helping them unlock a wealth of inspiration.

Drew's TEDx talk not only showcased his passion for music but also his ability to teach and guide in teaching others to become a singer/songwriter using his unique point of view. He demonstrated how songwriting can be a powerful tool for self-expression and encouraged individuals to embrace their unique stories and perspectives.

Through his genuine enthusiasm and heartfelt storytelling, Drew inspired countless individuals to explore the creative depths within themselves. By inviting them to embrace their life experiences and channel them into songwriting, he enabled them to tap into a powerful form of personal expression and connect with others on a deeper level.

Drew Lawrence's journey from passionate singer/songwriter to TEDx speaker exemplifies the transformative power of following one's passion. By sharing his love for songwriting and teaching others how to use their life stories as inspiration, he created a TEDx talk that resonated with audiences and empowered them to express themselves through the universal language of music.

You can check out Drew's talk at www.tedxhuntingtonbeach.com.

Success Actions

Here are simple success actions that you can do today to explore how your passion can lead to a TED-worthy idea:

1. Reflect on your passions and interests.
2. Write down one area that you're passionate about.

3. Set a timer for five minutes and create a mind map of anything that's associated with that area of interest that you can think of.

CHAPTER FIVE

Leverage Your Expertise - Illuminating the Path

"Seek the intersections where your knowledge meets universal themes or challenges to create your own unique take on an idea." - Dr. Izdihar Jamil

Leveraging your knowledge and experience can lead to the creation of a compelling talk that captivates, inspires, and sparks meaningful conversations. What's important to remember is that this is not the platform for you to promote your expertise to attract clients or generate sales- any form of marketing or promotion is strictly against the TED rules. What I'm guiding you towards is how your existing expertise can be leveraged in finding something that can lead to a new lesson or a unique idea that is a catalyst to impacting a community.

Let's explore how leveraging your expertise can pave the way for a remarkable TED-worthy idea.

Identify Your Unique Perspective

Your expertise grants you a unique lens through which to view the world. By identifying your distinctive viewpoint within your field, you can offer fresh insights and novel approaches to prevalent issues. Uncover the aspects that differentiate your expertise and explore how they can shed new light on a subject, capturing the attention and curiosity of the TED audience.

Share Your Passion

Your expertise is likely rooted in your passion for a particular subject. TED talks are most impactful when delivered with enthusiasm and genuine excitement. By infusing your passion into your talk, you can create an engaging and authentic connection with the audience. Your enthusiasm will be contagious, inspiring listeners to embrace your ideas and embark on their own intellectual journey.

Find the Intersection of Expertise and Universal Appeal

While your expertise may be specialized, it is important to identify the aspects that hold broader relevance. Seek the intersections where your knowledge meets universal themes or challenges. This ensures that your TED-worthy idea has the potential to resonate with diverse audiences, sparking curiosity and inspiring action beyond your specific field.

Provide Tangible Takeaways

A TED-worthy idea should not only be intellectually stimulating but also provide practical value to the audience. Consider how you can distill your expertise into tangible takeaways that attendees can apply to their own lives. Whether it's offering actionable steps, presenting tools or frameworks, or sharing personal anecdotes that inspire reflection, providing concrete and practical insights enhances the impact of your idea.

Embrace Authenticity and Vulnerability

TED talks thrive on authentic storytelling. Don't shy away from sharing personal experiences, challenges, or even failures that have shaped your expertise. By embracing vulnerability and authenticity, you establish a deep connection with the audience. This emotional resonance ensures that your talk leaves a lasting impact, as listeners relate to the human journey behind the expertise.

I encourage you to leverage your expertise to craft a TED-worthy idea that combines unique perspectives, passion, universal appeal, tangible takeaways, and authentic storytelling. By drawing upon your expertise, you have the power to share transformative ideas and inspire audiences around the globe. Embrace the opportunity to make a meaningful contribution, as your expertise holds the potential to shape minds, ignite change, and leave a lasting impact.

Guidelines to Brainstorm Your TED-worthy Idea Using Your Expertise

Here is a simple guideline on how you can leverage their expertise to develop a TED-worthy idea that captivates and inspires audiences.

Most Common Problems That You Solve

Reflect on the most common problems or challenges within your field that you have successfully addressed. Consider how your expertise, insights, or unique approaches have brought about transformative solutions. By identifying these recurring issues, you can shape your TED-worthy idea around providing valuable insights and practical solutions.

One Area of Your Expertise That Has a Significant Proven Track Record

Focus on a specific area of your expertise where you have a significant track record of success. Highlight the milestones, achievements, or breakthroughs you have attained in this particular domain. Most importantly, highlight the key lessons that you learned that can help others through your expertise. Remember, TEDx talk is about teaching people something new, different or specific- it's not about bosting your success. This can help you to position yourself as a credible authority and create a compelling foundation for your TED-worthy idea.

A Particular Failure That You or Your Client Has Experienced

Failure is often a catalyst for growth and learning. Share a specific failure or setback that you or your client encountered within your area of expertise. Detail the lessons learned, the insights gained, and how this experience transformed your approach or understanding. By showcasing vulnerability and the ability to overcome adversity, you humanize your expertise and connect with the audience on a deeper level.

Something That is Often Overlooked in Your Area of Expertise

Identify a commonly overlooked aspect within your field that, when addressed, can lead to a significant change or a better outcome for the community. Highlight the importance of this overlooked element and explain how incorporating this simple change can bring about transformative results. By shedding light on these often-underestimated factors, you challenge conventional wisdom and offer fresh perspectives to the TED audience.

Predicting a Solution 10 Years from Now

Leverage your expertise to envision a solution or anticipate a significant development that will shape the future of your field. Consider emerging trends, cutting-edge technologies, or innovative methodologies that have the potential to revolutionize your area of expertise. By sharing your forward-thinking insights and predictions, you stimulate curiosity and engage the audience in envisioning a future that is yet to unfold.

You can use their expertise to develop a TED-worthy idea by focusing on the problems they solve, emphasizing areas with proven track records, sharing failures and lessons learned, highlighting overlooked aspects, and providing forward-thinking solutions. By leveraging their expertise in these ways, you can create talks that inspire, educate, and spark transformative change.

Case Study

Aiko Hemingway's journey from Japan to the United States became the catalyst for her TEDx talk, driven by her expertise and passion for chasing her dream. Despite facing years of obstacles in pursuing her musical aspirations due to language barriers, Aiko embarked on a quest to find a solution that would enable her to express herself through effectively communicating with others in the English language.

Let's look into how Aiko developed her TEDx idea by leveraging her expertise.

Aiko's passion for music propelled her to explore unconventional techniques that could bridge the gap between language and self-expression. Through her relentless pursuit, she discovered that by altering vibrations and energy and refining her breathing techniques, Aiko unlocked the ability to pronounce challenging English words she previously struggled with, like the word "ear" instead of "year."

It also helped her to understand the English language better and for others to understand her communication clearly. This breakthrough not only enhanced her language skills but also unlocked a new avenue for her to communicate effectively.

With her newfound expertise, Aiko embarked on a mission to help other Japanese individuals struggling with English pronunciation. Through her TEDx talk, she shares her knowledge, teaching others how to utilize vibrations and breathing techniques to achieve native-like pronunciation. Aiko empowers adults to express themselves confidently and authentically in a foreign language.

Aiko's TEDx talk serves as a valuable resource for Japanese speakers seeking to overcome pronunciation challenges and find their voice in English. By imparting her expertise and sharing her personal journey, Aiko inspires others to embrace innovative techniques and overcome linguistic barriers. Her talk serves as a testament to the resilience and determination required to pursue one's passion.

Aiko Hemingway's TEDx idea emerged from her personal struggle with language barriers. Through her dedication and exploration, she discovered a unique technique, enabling her to improve her pronunciation skills and communicate effectively.

By sharing her expertise through her TEDx talk, Aiko empowers others to embrace this unique technique, opening doors for improved communication and self-expression. Her story serves as a testament to the transformative impact of leveraging one's expertise to overcome obstacles and inspire others along the way.

You can check out Aiko's talk at www.ted xhuntingtonbeach.com.

Success Actions

Here are simple success actions that you can do today to explore how you can use your expertise to lead to a TED-worthy idea:

1. Reflect on your expertise.
2. Write down one part of your expertise that you are passionate about or a part of your expertise that you consistently helped people solve.
3. Write down one simple, unique, or different solution that you can offer people from your experience of helping others.

CHAPTER SIX

Socio-Cultural Trends or Challenges - Riding the Waves of Change

"Observing socio-cultural trends can give you valuable clues to craft a unique TEDx talk."
- Dr. Izdihar Jamil

Recognizing the power of tapping into current socio-cultural challenges or trends when developing a TED-worthy idea can help you find a thought-provoking idea that is worth sharing. By offering unique, specific, or different solutions to these pressing issues, you can ignite meaningful discussions, inspire change, and create a lasting impact.

It is crucial to identify the socio-cultural challenges or trends that resonate deeply with the audience. Delve into topics that evoke strong emotions, spark debates, or impact people's daily lives. By understanding the pulse of society, speakers can frame their ideas in a context that is relevant and engaging to the audience.

Next, you should seek to offer a unique, specific, or different solution to these challenges or trends. This entails going beyond generic or conventional approaches and providing fresh perspectives, innovative strategies, or unexplored avenues. By offering a distinct solution, speakers stand out and captivate the audience's attention.

It is essential to back up the proposed solution with credible evidence, research, or personal experiences. By providing supporting data, case studies, or examples, speakers strengthen their credibility and establish a foundation for their ideas. The audience will be more likely to embrace the solution when it is rooted in evidence and expertise.

Clearly articulate why the proposed approach matters, how it can make a difference, and the potential positive outcomes it can bring. By highlighting the importance and potential impact of the solution, speakers can generate enthusiasm and inspire action.

You should approach their topic with empathy, sensitivity, and inclusivity. Recognize the diverse perspectives and experiences within the socio-cultural landscape and ensure that the proposed solution considers and respects various viewpoints. By fostering a sense of understanding and inclusiveness, speakers can create an environment that encourages dialogue, collaboration, and positive change.

Leveraging the current socio-cultural challenges or trends allows speakers to develop TED-worthy ideas that address pressing issues and offer unique, specific, or different solutions. By tapping into the pulse of society, supporting their ideas with evidence, emphasizing the importance of their solution, and approaching their topic with empathy, speakers can create talks that resonate with the audience and inspire meaningful action. TED provides a platform to showcase these innovative ideas and ignite conversations that shape the future of our society.

Guidelines to Explore Socio-Cultural Impact

By following a step-by-step guideline, you can effectively navigate this process and craft impactful talks that resonate with the audience.

Observe Any Persisting Trends
Begin by keenly observing the current socio-cultural landscape. Identify recurring patterns, emerging issues, or evolving trends that capture your attention. Pay close attention to topics that spark conversations, trigger debates, or significantly impact society. These trends serve as fertile ground for developing compelling TED-worthy ideas.

Research Those Trends
Conduct in-depth research to gain a deeper understanding of the identified trends. Explore existing literature, data, and expert opinions to gather comprehensive insights. Uncover the underlying

causes, consequences, and implications of these trends. This research phase provides a solid foundation for developing a well-informed TED-worthy idea.

Speak with the Community Involved with Those Trends

Engage with the community directly impacted by the identified trends. Listen to their stories, experiences, and perspectives. Conduct interviews, attend relevant events or forums, and immerse yourself in their world. This interaction helps you gain firsthand insights, empathy, and a nuanced understanding of the challenges faced by individuals within the community.

Link with Any Possible Socio-Cultural Impact

Analyze the broader socio-cultural impact of the identified trends. Examine how these trends influence different aspects of society, such as education, economy, environment, or human rights. Identify potential gaps, controversies, or opportunities for positive change. Connecting your idea to the socio-cultural impact strengthens its relevance and significance.

Explore Possible Solutions

Brainstorm innovative solutions that address the identified trends. Think outside the box and seek fresh perspectives. Consider how your expertise, experiences, or research can contribute to tackling these challenges. Identify unique approaches, methodologies, or insights that have the potential to inspire and empower the audience. Craft your idea around teaching the audience something new, different, or unique, enabling them to embrace or break through the identified trends.

By observing trends, conducting research, engaging with the community, linking with socio-cultural impact, and exploring unique solutions, thought leaders can develop TED-worthy ideas that are relevant, insightful, and inspiring. Embracing the TED platform provides an exceptional opportunity to share these ideas and catalyze positive change in society.

Case Study

As a case study, let's explore how Katya who spoke at TEDxHuntingtonBeach 2023 utilized the social distancing trend during the pandemic to develop a TED-worthy idea. Katya found herself facing the significant challenge of self-isolation, which led her to embark on a journey of seeking small, everyday sources of joy. By adopting what she calls the "treasure hunt framework," she discovered a unique perspective that she believed could positively impact others.

During the pandemic, when many were confined to their homes, Katya ventured out and purposefully sought out simple, everyday yet meaningful experiences. Whether it was observing the radiant shine of the sun or admiring the vibrant hue of a flower, she found joy in these small, everyday moments. Inspired by her own transformation, Katya realized that she had stumbled upon something powerful that could enhance the well-being of others.

In her TED-worthy idea, Katya introduces the concept of being a "treasure hunter" in the pursuit of joy. She encourages individuals to shift their focus from grand gestures or extraordinary occasional events to the beauty and joy that can be found in the everyday and ordinary life. By practicing mindfulness and actively engaging with their surroundings, you can uncover hidden treasures of happiness in their daily lives.

Katya's idea resonates with the social distancing trend during the pandemic as well as post pandemic, as it provides individuals with an alternative way to navigate the challenges of isolation and limited social interactions. By embracing the treasure hunt framework, people can cultivate a greater appreciation for the simple pleasures around them, fostering a sense of connection, gratitude, and fulfillment.

Through her TEDx talk, Katya aims to inspire and empower others to adopt this mindset of treasure hunting. By sharing her personal experiences, practical tips, and the transformative impact it has had on her own well-being, she offers a fresh perspective on finding joy amidst challenging times.

Katya leveraged the social distancing trend during the pandemic to develop her TED-worthy idea centered around the treasure hunt framework. By encouraging individuals to seek out and appreciate the small, everyday joys, she provides a valuable tool for navigating self-isolation and finding happiness even in the most challenging circumstances.

You can check out Katya's talk at www.ted xhuntingtonbeach.com.

Success Actions

Here are simple success actions on tapping into the current socio-cultural trends or challenges to lead to a TED-worthy idea:

1. Observe persisting, consistent, or small trends that are happening in the society or the community.
2. Write down one of those trends that you resonate with.
3. Set your timer for five minutes and create a mind map on the key points that you have identified with that trend.

CHAPTER SEVEN

Overcoming Adversity - Turning Pain into Power

"Your life story in overcoming adversity is filled with unique and valuable lessons. It's an opportunity to teach others something new." - Dr. Izdihar Jamil

Reflecting on your own life journey, challenges, and unique experiences can lead to compelling narratives that inspire and resonate with others. Here's why tapping into personal experiences can be a powerful strategy:

Authenticity

TED and TEDx talks thrive on authenticity and genuine storytelling. By exploring your own story, you bring a level of authenticity that connects deeply with the audience. Sharing personal experiences allows you to speak from a place of truth, which enhances the credibility and relatability of your talk.

Resonance

Personal stories have the ability to touch people's hearts and minds. When you share your journey of overcoming adversity, you create a profound connection with others who may have faced similar challenges. Your experiences can offer insights, hope, and inspiration, fostering a sense of empathy and understanding among the audience as well as taking bold actions that can create an impact.

Inspiration

Personal stories have the power to inspire and motivate others. By sharing how you navigated through difficult times, conquered obstacles, or embraced transformation, you provide a roadmap for others facing their own challenges. Your journey becomes a source of encouragement, showing that resilience, determination, and growth are possible even in the face of adversity.

Unique perspective

Your personal experiences are inherently unique. They offer a distinct lens through which you view the world and can provide fresh insights into universal themes or issues. By sharing your unique perspective, you contribute to the diversity of ideas within the TED community, offering a valuable and distinctive voice.

Even though your adversity may have a similar theme to others, the circumstances and how you approached things are different from others. One of the most common themes that I received as the Curator for TEDxHuntingtonBeach is tragedy.

After losing her home, her job, and the love of her life, Anjani took a spin on tragedy by encouraging others to stop, pause, and do something different. Often, when things start to happen, we would either keep going or have a huge breakdown. Also, when we do the same things over and over again, it can lead to the same result. But stop what we're doing, taking a pause and do something different it can help us to gain a different perspective. In Anjani's case, going to her first meditation, something that she has never done before helped to give her clarity on the most important thing and how she can move forward in her life at difficult times.

Laura used her unique perspective of surviving two floods, raccoons, and a fire at her house by inserting humor and her F.R.I.E.S. method to help others deal with trauma. Her F.R.I.E.S. method stands for:

F- Follow the clues and signs.
R- Reflect on the meaning behind events.
I – Intuitevely trust that meaning
E- Embrace the experience.
S- Stay open and curious.

By taking your unique point of view and lessons learned from your personalized adversity, you can help to teach others something new, different, or specific- just like Anjani and Laura.

Empowerment

Personal stories have the potential to empower individuals to take bold, courageous, and inspired actions. By highlighting your own journey, you can inspire others to embrace their own stories, find their voice, and make a positive impact. Your TED talk can serve as a catalyst for personal growth, encouraging individuals to step outside their comfort zones and pursue their dreams.

In my TEDx talk, "Coming to America: A Story of A Hijab Wearing Woman," I delivered a powerful message so that my nine-year-old daughter, Nadrah, can live in a world as a proud Muslim woman. I wanted to create a world where our society is open, accepting, and understanding of each other's differences.

Using my personal story of adversity, where someone left a bag of dog waste on our doorstep for Nadrah and me to discover. My unique TEDx idea that I shared was that the resolution to overcoming social adversity isn't to change or conform to the preconceived notions of society's checklist. As my call to action, I invited the audience to be proud of their roots and heritage as the solution to overcoming adversity and going against society's prejudice.

I have received many messages from people all around the world on how they could relate to my idea because they have experienced something similar. My strong call to action has inspired them to take bold, courageous actions in their life that are the opposite of society's culture and norms. Some of them took the brave action of sharing their voice in their TEDx talk.

Leveraging personal experiences in overcoming adversity is a powerful way to generate TEDx-worthy ideas. Reflecting on your own life journey, challenges, and unique experiences allows you to bring authenticity, resonance, inspiration, a unique perspective, and empowerment to your talk. By sharing personal stories that inspire and resonate with others, you contribute to the rich tapestry of TED talks and leave a lasting impact on the audience.

Guidelines on Exploring Personal Adversity

Here is a step-by-step guideline on how you can leverage their personal adversities to craft compelling TEDx talks:

The Lowest Point in Your Life

Reflect on the darkest and most challenging moments you have experienced. Identify the personal adversity that tested your resilience and pushed you to the brink. Consider the emotions, struggles, and lessons learned during this time.

The Biggest Failure

Examine a significant failure or setback you have encountered. This failure could have been a turning point in your life, forcing you to reevaluate your path and redefine your goals. Reflect on the valuable insights and growth that emerged from this experience.

Relate your Personal Adversity to Others

Connect your personal adversity to the broader human experience. Identify common themes, emotions, and struggles that others may resonate with. Consider how your journey can provide solace, hope, or guidance to individuals facing similar challenges.

Teach Something Unique from your Adversity

Determine what unique lessons or perspectives you can offer from your personal adversity. Consider the skills, strategies, or mindset shifts that helped you navigate through the adversity and ultimately overcome it. Focus on what you can teach others that they may not have encountered before.

Offer an Inspired Call to Action

Craft an inspiring call to action that encourages and empowers your audience to take action based on the insights gained from your adversity. Motivate them to apply the lessons learned to their own lives, fostering personal growth and resilience. Your call to action should leave the audience inspired, motivated, and equipped to make positive changes.

By following these steps, you can effectively leverage their personal and painful adversities to develop TEDx-worthy ideas. Sharing authentic stories of personal transformation, lessons learned, and practical advice creates a powerful connection with the audience. By offering unique teachings and an inspired call to action, thought leaders can leave a lasting impact, inspiring individuals to overcome their own challenges and embrace personal growth.

Remember, the path from personal adversity to a TEDx-worthy idea requires vulnerability, reflection, and a commitment to sharing your story in a way that resonates and inspires. By following these steps, you can harness the power of your own journey to create a compelling and transformative TED talk.

Case Study

Selina Lopez's journey from addiction, mental illness, and alcoholism to a life of sobriety became the foundation of her TEDx-worthy idea. Over the course of 20 years, she battled with the constant fear of whether each day would be her last- the day that she would give in to her addiction. In her TEDx talk, Selina shared her personal story and proposed a powerful solution to break the cycle of addiction and embrace a life of sobriety.

Selina's talk began by painting a vivid picture of the depths of her struggles and the desperation she felt. By sharing her lowest moments, she engaged the audience and created a connection based on shared vulnerability. She then revealed her personal turning point, the realization that she couldn't continue on this destructive path.

The unique aspect of Selina's idea emerged as she delved into her of creating a life of possibility- a life without addiction, when she suddenly had the urge to pick up the Bible. As she was flipping through the pages, she found a line that sternly warned her about the consequences of drinking alcohol. This warning became a catalyst for change for Selina and served as a powerful motivator to commit to a healthier and happier life.

Selina's TEDx talk offered a vision of a seemingly impossible future for addicts—a life of sobriety. Through her own transformation, she demonstrated that change is possible even after years of addiction. Her personal story became a source of inspiration and hope for others who may be caught in similar cycles.

By drawing on her own journey and the pain she caused her loved ones, Selina provided a unique perspective on addiction recovery. She taught the audience the importance of seeking support, acknowledging the impact of their actions, and, most importantly, how she keeps a life of sobriety by not letting herself be comfortable.

Her TEDx talk left the audience with an inspired call to action—to examine their own lives, relationships, and patterns of behavior and to take steps towards breaking destructive cycles and embracing a healthier, more fulfilling life while doing things that will expand their comfort zone consistently.

Selina Lopez's TEDx talk is a testament to the power of personal experiences in overcoming adversity and inspiring change. By sharing her story, she not only offered hope to those struggling with addiction but also encouraged individuals to reflect on their own challenges and take steps toward a brighter future.

Success Actions

Here are simple success actions on how you can use personal experience in overcoming adversity to lead to a TED-worthy idea:

1. List down one of your biggest adversity or failures.
2. Explore three things that you've learned from this adversity.
3. Write down one lesson or idea that the community can benefit from your adversity.

CHAPTER EIGHT

Challenging Assumptions and Thinking Disruptively - Breaking Chains of Thoughts

"Look beyond conventional wisdom. In finding your unique idea, look for something that is counterintuitive and can challenge society's normal thinking." - Dr. Izdihar Jamil

I encourage you to break away from conventional thinking patterns and embrace disruptive thinking to come up with a TEDx-worthy idea. The essence of a TEDx talk lies in challenging assumptions, questioning established norms, and pushing the boundaries of our imagination. Here's why thinking disruptively is essential.

Challenge Assumptions

Start by questioning the assumptions that underpin your field or topic of interest. Challenge the status quo and ask yourself, "Why do things have to be this way?" By questioning deeply ingrained beliefs, you open up new possibilities and uncover innovative solutions that may have been overlooked.

Embrace "What if" Questions

Explore alternative scenarios and imagine what could be possible if existing constraints were removed. "What if" questions inspire creative thinking and help you break free from the limitations of traditional approaches. Allow yourself to dream big and consider audacious ideas that have the potential to transform the way we perceive and interact with the world.

Explore Alternative Perspectives

Step into the shoes of different stakeholders, cultures, or disciplines. Adopting diverse perspectives allows you to see problems from new angles and gain fresh insights. Look beyond your comfort zone and seek inspiration from fields unrelated to your own. Cross-pollination of ideas often leads to breakthrough innovations and unexpected connections.

Envision Radical Solutions

Don't be afraid to think big and propose bold, disruptive solutions. TEDx-worthy ideas often challenge the existing paradigms and offer transformative approaches to longstanding problems. Push the boundaries of what is considered possible and strive to make a significant impact with your idea.

By thinking disruptively and challenging assumptions, you can unlock new avenues of creativity and generate TEDx-worthy ideas that captivate and inspire audiences. Remember, innovation thrives when we dare to question, explore, and envision a future that is different from the present. So, break free from the constraints of conventional thinking, embrace disruptive ideas, and share your unique perspective with the world through a TEDx talk that challenges assumptions and sparks meaningful change.

Guidelines on Challenging Assumptions and Thinking Disruptively

Here is a step-by-step guideline to help you navigate this process.

Look at Existing Assumptions

Begin by identifying the prevailing assumptions and beliefs within your field or topic of interest. Examine the underlying principles and norms that guide current thinking. Question why these assumptions have become ingrained and consider their potential limitations or biases.

Think About Opposites or What is Out of the Ordinary

Once you have identified the existing assumptions, deliberately explore the opposite or unconventional perspectives. Challenge yourself to think beyond the boundaries of what is considered "normal" or accepted. Ask yourself, "What if the opposite were true?" This exercise helps break free from conventional thinking and opens up new possibilities.

Look at Examples from History

Study historical events, breakthrough innovations, or paradigm shifts that have challenged prevailing assumptions. Analyze how disruptive thinkers of the past have reshaped our understanding of the world. Seek inspiration from their journeys and learn from their approaches to challenge existing beliefs.

Clarify the Importance of Challenging Assumptions

Clearly articulate why it is essential to challenge these assumptions and how doing so can benefit society. Highlight the potential limitations or drawbacks of adhering to conventional thinking. Emphasize the need for fresh perspectives and innovative ideas to address complex problems and drive positive change.

Provide Evidence of Disruptive Thoughts Leading to a Better Solution

Back up your arguments with evidence and examples that demonstrate how disruptive thinking has led to significant advancements or breakthroughs in your field. Show how challenging assumptions has paved the way for more effective solutions, improved outcomes, or positive societal impact.

By following these steps, you can challenge existing assumptions and embrace disruptive thinking to develop TEDx-worthy ideas. Remember, the power of a TEDx talk lies in questioning the status quo and presenting innovative perspectives that have the potential to revolutionize our understanding of the world. So dare to challenge assumptions, explore the unconventional, and share your disruptive thoughts with the world through a compelling TED talk.

Case Study

Anjani Amriit is a thought leader who fearlessly challenged existing assumptions and disrupted conventional thinking to develop her TEDx-worthy idea. In her thought-provoking TEDx talk, she boldly proposed that to create true innovation, one must transcend the boundaries imposed by the laws of physics and common law.

Anjani recognized that if humanity adhered strictly to the laws of physics that govern our world, we would never have been able to defy gravity and invent airplanes. She urged her audience to consider that true progress and groundbreaking ideas often emerge when we stretch our thinking beyond the confines of established norms.

Drawing from her personal journey, Anjani shared how she experienced the limitations of following the assumed trajectory of her legal career. As an overworked and burned-out lawyer, she realized that conforming to conventional wisdom and societal expectations was stifling her ability to live a meaningful and fulfilling life. It was only when she tapped into her higher intelligence and dared to challenge the existing assumptions about her career path that she found true inspiration and fulfillment.

Anjani's TEDx idea is a powerful call to action for individuals to harness their higher intelligence and break free from the constraints of conventional thinking. She emphasized that true innovation and progress often arise when we dare to explore new possibilities beyond what is deemed possible or accepted. By encouraging her audience to embrace disruptive thinking and challenge existing assumptions, Anjani believes we can unlock our potential to create meaningful change in our lives and society.

Anjani's journey serves as an inspiration for others who may feel trapped within the limitations of their chosen paths or societal expectations. Her message resonates with those who yearn for a more fulfilling and purpose-driven existence. By challenging existing assumptions and thinking disruptively, Anjani encourages individuals to tap into their higher intelligence and create a future that defies the boundaries of what is currently perceived as possible.

Through her TEDx talk, Anjani Amriit offers a powerful reminder that the path to innovation and personal fulfillment lies in questioning assumptions, pushing boundaries, and embracing the potential of our higher intelligence to shape a better and more meaningful future.

Success Actions

Here are simple success actions on how you can challenge existing assumptions and embrace disruptive thinking to lead to a TED-worthy idea:

1. Identify one area in which you would like to challenge the existing assumptions.
2. List the current assumptions in this area.
3. Think "What if" and start to explore disruptive solutions to this area.

CHAPTER NINE

Physical Limitations - Beyond Boundaries

"Reflecting on physical limitations can create an opener to a profound and meaningful TEDx idea. It's all about exploring what's possible!"
- Dr. Izdihar Jamil

Physical limitations do not define the breadth of our potential. Rather, they serve as catalysts for innovation, resilience, and creativity. They can be used as powerful sources of inspiration and impact.

What's Possible

See what's possible beyond the physical limitations: Instead of viewing physical limitations as barriers, leaders must adopt a mindset that explores the uncharted territories of possibility. By shifting our perspective, we can uncover hidden strengths, skills, and perspectives that would otherwise remain untapped. Look beyond the confines of what seems impossible and envision new horizons waiting to be explored.

Key Lessons

Draw out key lessons from physical limitations: Physical limitations offer profound lessons that can shape our leadership journey. Embrace the challenges, setbacks, and adaptations required by your limitations. These experiences nurture resilience, empathy, and a deep understanding of human potential. Recognize that our limitations can teach us valuable lessons that transcend the physical realm and serve as pillars of wisdom to guide our actions.

Positive Propeller

See the physical limitation as a positive propeller towards something greater: Rather than perceiving physical limitations as roadblocks, be open to viewing them as propellers towards something greater. Our limitations can ignite a fire within us, inspiring us to create meaningful change, advocate for inclusion, and challenge societal norms. Let your physical limitation become a powerful driving force to fuel your determination, ignite your passion, and motivate you to contribute to a better world.

When you harness the power of their physical limitations, you unlock boundless potential. We can transcend the boundaries of what is perceived as possible by seeing beyond the limits, drawing lessons from adversity, and leveraging limitations as propellers toward greatness. Together, let us embrace our physical limitations and transform them into

TEDx-worthy ideas that ignite positive change, inspire others, and redefine the notion of leadership.

Guidelines for Using Physical Limitations to Brainstorm TED-Worthy Ideas

Let us explore the key points that will guide you in harnessing the power of your physical limitations to create a transformative TED-worthy idea.

Beyond Limitation

What has the physical limitation enabled you to do? Reflect on how your physical limitation has shaped your journey and enabled you to accomplish remarkable feats. Embrace the unique perspective it has granted you and the insights it has offered into the human experience. Recognize that your physical limitation serves as a powerful tool to connect with others and inspire change.

Mindset Shift

What mindset shift have you had to adapt to embrace your physical limitation? Embracing a mindset shift is crucial in harnessing the potential of your physical limitation. Shift your focus from what you cannot do to what you can achieve despite your limitations. Embrace resilience, adaptability, and an unwavering belief in your abilities. By embracing a physical limitation as a part of your identity, you can uncover new avenues for personal growth and innovation.

Areas of Achievements

List out five areas in which you have achieved by embracing your physical limitations. Demonstrate the myriad ways in which you have triumphed over adversity and achieved remarkable success despite your physical limitations. Highlight your professional accomplishments, personal growth, community contributions, and any groundbreaking innovations that have emerged from your unique perspective. Showcase the limitless possibilities that can arise when one embraces their physical limitations.

Outside Feedback

What have others told you about your physical limitations? Share the insights and feedback you have received from others regarding your physical limitations. Discuss how their perspectives have shaped your journey and how their encouragement and support have fueled your determination. Showcasing the positive impact you have had on others can inspire and empower the audience to reframe their own perceptions of limitations.

What People Don't Know

What do you want others to know about your physical limitation and the possibility it created in your life? Leave the audience with a profound understanding of the potential that lies within physical limitations. Communicate the message that limitations do not define a person, but rather provide a unique opportunity for growth, resilience, and innovation. Encourage individuals to view their own limitations as powerful tools for self-discovery and to embrace the possibilities that arise from embracing their uniqueness.

By embracing your physical limitations and utilizing them as a springboard for personal and professional growth, you can unlock a world of possibilities. Embrace the mindset shift, celebrate your achievements, and inspire others to challenge their own limitations. Together, let us transform our physical limitations into TEDx-worthy ideas that ignite change, redefine societal norms, and inspire a future where limitations are seen as opportunities for greatness.

Case study

Patricia Bartell is a remarkable individual who has defied the odds and used her physical limitation as a catalyst for personal and professional growth. Patricia's story serves as a powerful case study on how one can embrace one's physical limitations to inspire others to take brave actions and create a life filled with possibility.

At a young age, Patricia was struck by polio, which left her with physical limitations. However, she refused to let her circumstances define her. Instead, she redefined the meaning of crutches, seeing them not as tools to limit her, but as instruments to propel her towards success. This mindset shift was the foundation of her extraordinary journey.

Embracing her crutches as a part of her leadership success, Patricia exemplifies resilience, determination, and an unwavering belief in her abilities. She has shattered societal norms and proven that physical limitations do not have to hinder one's dreams. Patricia's accomplishments as a world-champion accordionist and a successful entrepreneur are a testament to her unwavering spirit and refusal to be confined by her physical limitations.

Through her TEDx talk, Patricia shares her story with authenticity and vulnerability, inspiring others to embrace their own challenges and discover their limitless potential. She empowers individuals to break free from societal expectations and pursue their passions with unwavering courage and determination. Patricia's message resonates deeply with audiences as she encourages them to challenge their own limitations and redefine what is possible.

With her unique perspective and personal experiences, Patricia demonstrates that physical limitations can serve as a powerful driving force towards personal and professional success. Rather than asking yourself "What's wrong with me?", Patricia encouraged her audience to first ask the emotion that is connected with the question.

In her own reflection, the question of "What's wrong with me?" was tied to the emotion that she is not loved. Once you have identified the emotion, you can then choose to change the question that you ask yourself and the emotion that is tied with it.

Patricia said that once she has understood that, she stopped blaming her crutches for her misfortunes. She started to see that her crutches serve as a powerful tool for her to travel, to work, to play her music and guide others in building a successful business. Her story serves as a rallying cry for individuals to overcome adversity and embrace their uniqueness as a source of strength.

Patricia Bartell's remarkable journey stands as a shining example of how embracing physical limitations can inspire individuals to take brave actions and create a life of unlimited possibility. Her passion, resilience, and success are a testament to the human spirit's indomitable nature.

Her story is a beacon of hope and inspiration for us all using her crutches to take that step moving forward. In her own words, Patricia described her journey as "from crutches to crushing it". Through her TEDx talk, she encourages individuals to see beyond their physical limitations and embark on a journey of self-discovery, growth, and possibility. Let us all be inspired by Patricia's example and take brave actions towards creating lives filled with purpose and fulfillment.

Success actions

Here are simple success actions on how you can embrace physical limitations to lead to a TED-worthy idea:

1. List down five areas of achievements from your physical limitations.
2. In each area, explore how physical limitations have helped to propel you toward success or created something positive.
3. Write down one unique lesson or idea from those experiences.

CHAPTER TEN

Landing Your Dream TEDx Talk-Stand Out and Shine

"My TEDx talk started with a vision followed by bold, decisive actions, all while embracing fear and uncertainty." - Dr. Izdihar Jamil

In this chapter, I will guide you through the intricate process of securing that coveted spot on the TEDx stage. It's an endeavor that requires dedication, strategy, and a heartfelt connection with your message and with the organizers. So, let's get started.

Research Each Organizer and Event Thoroughly

Before you even think about crafting your pitch or reaching out, it's crucial to thoroughly research each TEDx event and organizer you're interested in. Head over to their website, immerse yourself in their content, and explore their social media presence. Try to get a sense of the event's theme, tone, and past speakers. Understanding their unique identity will allow you to tailor your approach and pitch to align seamlessly with their vision.

Make sure you also note any specific guidelines or requirements they have for potential speakers. This research is your foundation, and it's the first step in demonstrating your genuine interest in being part of their event.

For example, I've received several applications for TEDxHuntingtonBeach from speakers who clearly want to promote their own agenda- their books, their framework, their business but disguise it as their passion.

If they had done their research about TEDxHuntingtonBeach and me, they would know that our commitment Is to one thing and one thing only: creating a movement within the community with thought-provoking conversations and ideas. It's about something larger than one's ego, business, brand, or books. I wanted to create a world that's open and accepting so that Nadrah can grow up to be a proud Muslim woman.

This is not just for my daughter, Nadrah, but for my best friends' daughters and my neighbors' daughters. It is for moms who have daughters out there and want to create a better world for them so they can be proud of who they are and live in a society that is open and accepting of each other's differences.

Not only do those applications that are ego-centric waste a lot of my time and the team's time, but also they did not align themselves with the vision of TED-ideas worth spreading and becoming a catalyst for impact.

TEDx organizers are not paid. They are volunteers who are passionate about a vision of making an impact. So, the more you can make things easy for the organizer, the easier the process will be for you.

Understand What Each Organizer Is Looking For

Different TEDx events have distinct themes and goals. Some may be focused on technology and innovation, while others may center around social justice or the environment. It's essential to understand what each organizer is looking for in their speakers. Do your values, experiences, and ideas align with their mission? Does your story complement their theme? Are you the missing piece of their puzzle?

Remember, if an event is not actively seeking speakers or if their theme doesn't resonate with your message, it's best not to pitch. It's a two-way street; you should genuinely believe in the event's mission, and they should see the value you bring to their stage.

In reviewing the applications for TEDxHuntingtonBeach, one of the questions asked that they submit a one-minute video addressing specific content. I wanted to see if they could follow simple instructions and are coachable when doing the video.

You wouldn't believe the type of submissions that I received. There are people who submit their book trailer- which has nothing to do with their applications. There are people who submitted a 5 to 10-minute video. They are people who made a very general video, which they probably recorded and used to submit to several other organizers. There were people who didn't even follow the guidelines that were outlined to them.

Be clear on what the organizers are looking for, and be respectful and intentional with your submissions. This will reveal your character and will make a difference in helping you proceed to the next round.

Create a Relationship with the Organizer

Once you've identified an event and organizer that resonates with you, it's time to start building a relationship. Send a thoughtful email introducing yourself, your background, and your passion for their work. Explain why their event is the perfect platform for your message. Make it personal—show them that you've done your homework and that you genuinely admire what they're doing.

Additionally, follow the organizer on social media. Engage with their content, share their posts, and participate in conversations relevant to their mission. Building a relationship is about genuine connection, so be authentic and patient.

In the past, I've had people who commented on the majority of my posts and recorded videos sharing how they were inspired by my TEDx talk. I thought it was cool that they are supporting the vision, but it turns out they are not genuine about it. They are doing it because they wanted to get something from me. Once they got that something, they just disappeared.

If you truly want to create a relationship with someone, you do it without strings because the biggest currencies of business are RELATIONSHIP and TRUST. It can lead to so many amazing things once you've planted the right seeds for your vision.

See If You Are a Good Fit with One Another

Creating a relationship isn't just about convincing the organizer that you're a great fit for their event; it's also about discovering if the event aligns with your goals and message. Attend their events, if possible, engage with their community, and ask questions that help you understand their vision and expectations. Demonstrate how you can be an asset versus an adversary in the team. A strong partnership should benefit both parties, so make sure it's a good fit in terms of values, messaging, and mutual goals.

You will be on a journey and will be spending a few months together. Naturally, you want to work with the people that you like, who care about you, who are in alignment with your visions versus their own personal benefits and ego-based motivations.

TEDxDelthroneWomen and Sonali Fiske (the organizer) were a great fit for me! I wanted to be in a women's-based conference led by strong women. I love their theme- REVOLUTION, which is in full alignment with my TEDx idea of not conforming with society's preconceived notion but being faithful to your roots and heritage. Plus, it was less than an hour's drive from home- which was perfect because I got to come home to Rayhan, Abrar, and Nadrah.

Don't settle. Don't just apply to a TEDx event just because it's a numbers game. Apply because you are fully in alignment with the vision, the people, and their creation. You'll be spending months with them, so choose your the event, organizer and team surrounding yo carefully.

Submit Your Application When the Application Submissions Are Open

Timing is crucial in the TEDx world. Once you've done your research, built a relationship with the organizer, and confirmed that it's a good fit, the final step is to submit your application when they open their call for speakers. Follow their guidelines meticulously, and make sure your pitch reflects your authentic self and your unique message that aligns with the event's theme.

Remember, patience and persistence are key. The selection process can be highly competitive, but with your genuine interest and connection, the right timing, and a thoughtful pitch, you can increase your chances of landing that TEDx talk.

For TEDxHuntingtonBeach, I created a link for those who were interested in applying to drop their speaker details. I didn't want to be bombarded with hundreds of emails. Organizing TEDxHuntington Beach isn't the only thing that I do. I have three kids, a husband, a business, and community events. It is not an efficient use of my time to be answering minuscule emails, especially when there are clear instructions on how to proceed with the applications on our website. So, make sure you check the organizer's website and thoughtfully follow their instructions.

Once the application was opened, I sent an email out to those that registered in the mailing list. Equally as important, submit your application early or on time. DO NOT ask for an extension as this reveals your character. Events are time-critical, so make sure you are spot on with deadlines and timings.

Those who submitted late to TEDxHuntington Beach did not get to go in, nor were there any extensions. I wanted to work with people who value and respect the timeline of the event as well as the vision of the theme. This will help us to move in the same direction easily and effortlessly.

What Makes Your TEDx Application Stand Out?

Crafting a standout application is your ticket to the TEDx stage, and it's all about showcasing your unique blend of authenticity, vision, and commitment. After reviewing hundreds of TEDx applications, I've boiled down to several key things that can make your application stand out. Here's your guide to making a lasting impression:

Polish Your Digital Presence

Clean up your social media playground. Your online persona should radiate trust and align with the values of the TEDx brand. Craft a narrative that mirrors the honesty and openness you bring to the stage.

Build a Professional Digital Home

Your website gives a quick snapshot of your character, brand and what you're passionate about.

Ensure it reflects a clear vision and character. Let its design and messaging speak volumes about your TEDx-worthy ideas. A professional touch conveys dedication and seriousness about your message.

Align with the TEDx Theme

Resist the urge to chase popularity, money, or divisive agendas. Ensure your messaging harmonizes with the TEDx theme. This isn't about trends; it's about ideas that transcend, provoke thought, and inspire change.

Unveil Your Authentic Self

TEDx is about more than just ideas; it's about people. Showcase your multifaceted self – from family to community involvement, and passions. Let the audience see the real you, fostering connection and relatability.

Portray Your Best Character

Trust, credibility, and reliability are TEDx's bedrock. Highlight experiences that illustrate your character. Demonstrate how your journey uniquely equips you to share a message that matters.

Embrace Team Spirit

TEDx thrives on collaboration. Showcase instances where you've excelled as a team player. Your ability to contribute to a collective vision adds depth to your application.

Demonstrate Coachability

Be open to refinement. Show that you embrace feedback and value the collaborative process. TEDx speakers are lifelong learners; let your eagerness to grow shine through.

In your application, paint a picture that transcends words, a mosaic of your genuine self and compelling vision. Your story is the TEDx story—make it unforgettable!

Start building those meaningful connections and exploring the TEDx events that align with your mission. Your TEDx journey is just beginning, and the world is waiting to hear your inspiring message.

CHAPTER ELEVEN

5 Steps to Jumpstart Your TEDx Journey - Your Odyssey Begins

"Even up until today, I receive heartfelt messages from people around the world that told me how my TEDx talk inspired them to be bold and courageous in challenging the preconceived notions."
- Dr. Izdihar Jamil

The journey to delivering a TEDx talk is not just about standing on that iconic red circle; it's about igniting change and inspiring the world. In this chapter, we'll dive into the essential process of generating a TEDx-worthy idea and securing a spot on the coveted TEDx stage.

Step One: Brainstorm Your Idea

Brainstorming a truly exceptional idea is the first and most crucial step in your TEDx journey. Your idea should be like no other, unique, different, and specific—something that challenges norms, ignites curiosity, and has the potential to inspire transformation. Ask yourself, "What issue or concept am I truly passionate about? What can I share that people can learn from and spark thought-provoking conversations and will leave a lasting impact?"

Don't hold back; let your creativity soar. The most memorable talks often come from sharing personal stories, experiences, or novel insights. The key is choosing a subject that resonates deeply with you, something you genuinely believe in. Your enthusiasm will shine through and captivate your audience.

Step Two: Research Each Organizer and Event Thoroughly:

Your journey doesn't end with a great idea; it continues with understanding the context in which you'll be presenting it. Delve into each TEDx event and organizer you're interested in. Explore their website, social media profiles, and past speakers. Take the time to learn about their mission, values, and the themes they've covered in the past. Your goal is to understand their unique identity and narrative.

By conducting thorough research, you can ensure that your idea aligns seamlessly with the event's objectives and the expectations of its audience. The more you comprehend the organizer's world, the better you can craft a talk that resonates with their vision.

Step Three: Understand What Each Organizer Is Looking For:

Each TEDx event has its own set of criteria and expectations. It's paramount to understand what each organizer is seeking in their speakers, their theme, and their specific requirements. Contact the event organizers if you need clarification or have questions. Clear communication shows that you're thoughtful and dedicated but be mindful that you are not over-communicating. Be intentional and mindful with your communication to get your answers while respecting their boundaries.

Step Four: Submit Your Application When the Application Is Open

Timing is a critical factor in your TEDx journey. As soon as you've done the groundwork—researched the event, grasped their theme, and confirmed they are accepting speakers—submit your application when they open their call. Be prompt, and ensure you adhere to their guidelines to the letter. A well-prepared, timely submission showcases your professionalism and enthusiasm.

Pitching outside this window is likely to lead to disappointment, and some organizers may not even entertain it. Submitting your applications per the guidelines demonstrates your attention to detail and ability to follow instructions. It also showcases that you're a team player- working together to achieve a common goal.

If you did not get the spot to speak at TEDx events, reflect on what worked and what didn't work with your recent applications. Tweak your application to make it better. Then, repeat the process until you find the perfect fit. Many TEDx speakers, including myself, were rejected multiple times. But in those rejections, we learned valuable lessons and that made our applications stronger.

Step Five: Craft Your Talk and Rehearse

Once you secure your spot on the TEDx stage, it's time to shape your talk. It should be a masterpiece of storytelling, delivering your unique idea with precision and clarity. Remember, you have just 10 minutes or less to transform lives.

Even if you haven't secured your TEDx talk yet, start rehearsing now. Act as if it is already happening. Some TEDx organizers may ask for a video of your full talk, so this will get you prepared early and stand out from other applications because you have already rehearsed.

Begin with an engaging opening that captures your audience's attention, follow with a structured narrative that conveys your idea, and conclude with a powerful message that lingers long after the talk is over. Utilize personal anecdotes, data, and visuals to support your message, and, above all, be authentic. Your talk should mirror who you are and what you stand for.

Rehearse relentlessly. Practice in front of a mirror, record yourself, or seek feedback from friends and mentors. The more you rehearse, the more confident and comfortable you'll become. Instead of memorizing your talk verbatim, focus on understanding the structure and flow so you can speak from the heart.

Your TEDx talk is your chance to share your remarkable idea with the world. These five steps will guide you toward securing a spot and delivering a talk that inspires, empowers, and leaves a profound impact. Embrace your unique idea, embark on your research journey, and craft your talk with unwavering passion. Your TEDx journey is well underway. Follow the steps that I have laid out TODAY and keep moving forward in sharing your unique idea. I can't wait to see you speak on the TED stage!

Best wishes,
Izdihar

About the Author

Dr. Izdihar Jamil, Ph.D., is an immigrant, Asian, hijab-wearing Muslim computer scientist turned visibility expert. She is the curator and organizer for TEDxHuntingtonBeach and is instrumental in coaching many speakers for the TEDx stage. She is a 19 time #1 International Bestselling Author of *Money Makers*, *Women Who Lead,* and *Are You Visible?*

Izdihar has spoken at many prestigious events and interviews all around the world. She has her own TV Show aired on Apple TV, Amazon Fire TV, and ROKU called "It Takes COURAGE" where she features influential leaders discussing their success secrets.

She was featured on FORBES, TED.com, FOX TV, NBC, CBS, ABC, CW, *Thrive Global*, and hundreds of media and publications. She's the curator for TEDxHuntingtonBeach- sharing the voices of her community.

In 2021, Izdihar was inducted into the prestigious *Marquis Who's Who* biography to recognize her contribution as one of the top 5% in the industry alongside Warren Buffet and Oprah.

Her TEDx Talk on overcoming social adversity and the courage to be proud of your roots and heritage has inspired many people from various cultures to take a positive step in accepting other people's principles and values.

She is an influential trailblazer and an inspirational leader in helping leaders share their voices on prestigious platforms without prejudice.

She has helped hundreds of leaders to become bestselling authors and get featured in major media and TEDx stages with her simple, no-fuss visibility methods.

Izdihar lives in California with her husband and three kids, and in her spare time, she loves reading and baking for her family.

Also by Dr. Izdihar Jamil

You can enjoy other books by Izdihar, which are available on Amazon.

Money Makers

Possibility

The Confidence of Yes

Hello SUCCESS

Ambitious Women Rise

Feisty

She Made It Happen

Yes I Can! 22 Success Secrets From Inspiring People Around The World

Yes I Can! 15 Mindset Secrets From Successful Entrepreneurs Around The World

Yes I Can! 16 Success Secrets From Inspiring Women Around The World

She's A Boss

Hello SUCCESS Journal

Women Who Lead, Vol 1

Women Who Lead, Vol 2

It Is Done

FREEBIE

Want to write your bestselling book in 30 days?

Access the checklist here-
https://www.izdiharjamil.com/freebie
Or scan the QR code below.

www.ingramcontent.com/pod-product-compliance
Lightning Source LLC
Chambersburg PA
CBHW060324130626
46553CB00003B/910